Should We Wear School Uniforms?

by Mrs. Cervantes' class
with Tony Stead

capstone®
classroom

Should we wear uniforms to school? This is a question that our class has been debating. Some of the kids in our class think that uniforms should be worn to school. There are other kids in our class who think that uniforms are a bad idea. We are going to look at both sides of the argument. Then you can decide whether or not uniforms at school make sense!

The Case for School Uniforms

Do you want to wear uniforms for school? Sign me up! There have been many debates for and against school uniforms. But I think uniforms are a great idea.

First of all, uniforms can prevent bullying due to fashion. Some parents cannot buy expensive clothes for school. Other kids make fun of students who do not have good clothes.

Another reason in favor of uniforms is that uniforms can increase student commitment and teamwork. With uniforms, a more educational tone is set. That encourages students to take their homework more seriously.

Finally, clothing is something that might cause students to fight. Uniforms can stop those problems and lead to fewer detentions and suspensions in school.

by Melody

Bullying is a big problem in schools across the United States. One resource (*The Free Press*, Kingston, NC) conducted a survey on peer pressure. It found that more than 3.2 million students are victims of bullying, and 71 percent of students report incidents of bullying at their schools. I strongly believe that wearing uniforms to school can reduce these statistics. For example, wearing uniforms can make a student's economic differences less noticeable. Students should be focused on getting better grades and preparing for their futures. In order to learn, we need to feel safe and free from negative peer pressure. Dressing stylishly and wearing expensive clothes can put pressure on students. Uniforms can take that pressure away.

by Robert

Increased pride, unity, and a renewed commitment to the school—why would these be problems in school? They're not problems! With uniforms a more professional tone is set, encouraging students to take their studies more seriously. Kids are very friendly because they are social by nature, and they need to feel that they are part of a group—that they belong. Some students do not like to play with other kids. This makes those kids feel excluded, and it is very hard to learn when you are sad. Additionally, when there is unity in a school, students usually help each other out with school subjects and advice about school and life. Uniforms make a school like a second home. It becomes a place where you belong.

by Elyse

9

Statistics focused on school uniforms show that suspension dropped by 90 percent and fighting dropped by 38 percent when students were required to wear uniforms in Long Beach, California. This data supports the idea that wearing uniforms to school is a very good idea. I want to go to school where I feel safe. I want to be a doctor when I grow up. It's good to be in a school without fighting because everyone feels safe and I can focus on my studies. Uniforms make a school feel safe, and they are good for learning.

by David

11

Are uniforms a good idea? Of course, they are a great idea! School uniforms can help students be more respectful to one another. For example, peers will accept each other for who they really are and not for their clothes. Another good reason is money. School uniforms might cost parents about $240 a year, which is less than buying clothes throughout the school year. The last reason is that uniforms can reduce gangs on school campuses.

Peer pressure and fitting in by wearing expensive clothes is a big problem in schools today. Children compete to wear the expensive brands in the market. For instance, imagine Peter wears a really expensive outfit. But Bryan is not that lucky. Peter starts making jokes about Bryan's outfit. Bryan is unhappy because his peers buy $100 jeans from a top store, but his parents are not able to do so. He wears $10 jeans from another store. Adults need to understand firsthand that we feel better when the attention is not on how we look, but instead on our success in school and our grades.

Uniforms also are a cost savings that allow families to save money for unexpected emergencies. I remember not too long ago that my grandma got sick and needed urgent care. We needed to borrow money from family members to pay the bill. Therefore, a family that has to buy uniforms instead of a variety of clothes can save money for expenses like this.

There are many reasons to wear uniforms to school, such as respect and the savings that come with buying uniforms. But how about the reduction of violence in school? The last reason by itself is good enough for me to vote for uniforms! Would you like to wear a uniform to school?

by Amy

The Case Against School Uniforms

Uniforms for school? Who wants to wear one? Personally, I think this is not a good idea. First of all, you always hear parents complaining about kids' rooms being too messy. If students are choosing their own clothes, they have to think about what they are going to wear every day. Organization becomes really important, therefore kids' rooms become less messy. Another reason that uniforms are not a good idea is that they really do not prevent fights or violence.

Even when children are dressed the same, there will always be someone disturbing the peace in the classroom. Lastly, students need to express their unique individualism. Uniforms do just the opposite. Students need to grow up and be independent.

by Kevin

There aren't many schools that require kids to wear uniforms, and there are good reasons for this! I strongly believe that kids should not wear uniforms to school.

First of all, there's no reason to wear uniforms. Sometimes, my grandma says, "If it isn't broke, why fix it?" I agree! The clothes that we wear to school are fine. As long as kids wear clothes that don't distract other kids and are safe to wear to school, there's no reason to have a uniform.

Uniforms are also uncomfortable. Who wants to wear a shirt with a scratchy collar? Who wants to wear clothes that are too tight for us to run and play? I don't! I also know that a lot of uniforms for girls are skirts or dresses. I don't want to wear a skirt or dress every day. I'm more comfortable in pants or shorts. Uniforms just aren't comfortable for most students.

When students are uncomfortable, they can't focus on their schoolwork. And if the clothes we wear to school already are just fine, then why should we change? These reasons support my opinion. Uniforms aren't necessary! They don't belong in school.

by Renee

Organization is important to student success. Organization starts at home. We learn by doing our chores, cleaning our rooms, folding our school clothes, and separating the dark and white clothes from our hampers before we wash. Organization is going to be the key if your plan is a college degree. Having to choose clothes and organize clothes is a helpful skill for the future. Wearing uniforms takes this chance away.

I firmly believe that uniforms on their own will not prevent school violence. There will always be that one kid who bullies another over clothing, but that is not the real problem. We need better solutions, like resolving conflict so that we all get along and feel safe at school. Uniforms are just a bandage for a real problem.

We should express ourselves! Studies show that children's characters are formed at a very young age. We should have say-so in what we wear every day to better develop our personalities, independence, and confidence. Wearing uniforms to school does the opposite. For example, if we can't express ourselves freely, we might feel the need to rebel as we get older and choose the wrong type of clothes.

In order for students to learn, we need to feel safe from violence. If we want to get good grades, organization is very important. We need to grow up confident and independent and express who we are. For all these reasons, uniforms are not a good idea.

by Aisha

School is important. We need to learn and get good grades. We need to feel safe in school. We need to be around other people who want to cooperate and work together. Do uniforms make a school a better place to learn? You have heard lots of reasons for school uniforms and lots of reasons against them. What do you think about wearing uniforms to school?